IN THE FOOTSTEPS OF

DRACULA

JIM PIPE

COPPER BEECH BOOKS
BROOKFIELD, CONNECTICUT

Designed and produced by
Aladdin Books Ltd
28 Percy Street, London W1P 0LD

First published in 1995 in the United States by
Copper Beech Books, an imprint of
The Millbrook Press
2 Old New Milford Road
Brookfield, Connecticut 06804

Editor
Katie Roden
Designed by
David West Children's Book Design
Designer Flick Killerby
Picture Research Brooks Krikler Picture Research
Illustrators
Francesca D'Ottavi, Susanna Addario – McRae Books, Florence, Italy

Printed in Belgium

Library of Congress Cataloging-in-Publication Data
Pipe, Jim. 1966-
Dracula/Jim Pipe : illustrated by Francesca d'Ottavi and S. Addario.
p. cm. -- (In the Footsteps of - -)
Includes index.
ISBN 1-56294-646-3 (lib. bdg.). --ISBN 1-56294-186-0 (pbk.)
1. Vampires--Juvenile literature. [1. Vampires.] I. D'Ottavi, Francesca,
ill. II. Addario, Susanna, ill. III. Title. IV. Series.
GR830. V3P57 1995   95-13148 CIP
398.21--dc20   AC

CONTENTS

Bram Stoker's
DRACULA

It was a cold, clear night, and the moon shone down upon the inn. An icy gust of wind whistled up the stairs, under a door, and across a bare room. A candle flickered, lighting up the face of the lonely figure hunched over the table. Jonathan Harker gathered up the documents that would soon make Count Dracula the owner of Carfax House in London. The young lawyer had been sent to Transylvania to finish the sale. It was his first task since passing his exams, and he felt uneasy at the thought of meeting this mysterious client.

It had been a tiring day, and he had a long train journey ahead of him. Yawning, Harker shuffled across to the bed, the old floorboards creaking at every step. As he lay awake, gazing at a picture of his beautiful wife Mina, the howling of wolves echoed in the distance. Little did he know they were calling out to welcome him...

20 April. Bistritz – Left Munich at 8.35 p.m. on 18 April, arriving at Vienna early next morning, should have arrived at 6.45, but train was an hour late. Buda-Pesth seems a wonderful place, from the glimpse which I got of it from the train and the little I could walk through the streets. I feared to go very far from the station, as we had arrived late and would start as near the correct time as possible. We left in pretty good time, and came after nightfall to Klausenburgh. Here we stopped for the night at the Hotel. I had for dinner, or rather supper, a chicken done up some way with red

INTRODUCTION

I, Count Dracula, Prince of Darkness, bid you welcome. Come, follow in my footsteps and you will find there is more to me than meets the eye. For I am part history, part imagination – and all evil!

A World of Terror

My terrifying story takes you to Transylvania, the mystical "land beyond the forests," and my home for 500 years. Let me introduce you to Vlad the Impaler, my bloodthirsty ancestor, and to Countess Bathory, who once bathed in the blood of young women. Meet my terrible cousins from around the world, from green demons in ancient China to vampire watermelons in Bosnia!

Discover the secrets of bats and my other bloodsucking friends, and learn about my amazing powers of hypnosis. Last but not least, I offer a few hints on what to do if you are ever unlucky enough to meet me in person!

Bram Stoker, Vampire Author

The story in this book is based on Bram Stoker's novel *Dracula*, written in 1897.

Born in 1847, Stoker (*left*) was a sickly child who spent the first eight years of his life confined to bed. Here his mother told him tales of the plague, which inspired him to write his horror classic. Whether there is any truth in his writing, I cannot tell you, but I hope you enjoy my story. Yours eternally,

Count Dracula

The next morning, Harker watched the beautiful Transylvanian countryside as it drifted past. At Bistritz, a coach was waiting for him. Climbing inside, Harker met a merchant and his family on their way to visit relatives across the mountains. Soon the coach was trundling along muddy roads, and the family whispered excitedly to each other in their native Romanian. Now and then, they glanced up at the stranger with fear in their eyes.

As the coach neared the Borgo Pass, the mother could restrain herself no longer. She turned to Harker and pleaded: "Young man, it is St. George's Eve. Do you not know that when the clock strikes midnight tonight, all evil things are at their most powerful?" Taking a crucifix from her neck, she offered it to him: "If you must go on, then for your mother's sake, wear this at all times..."

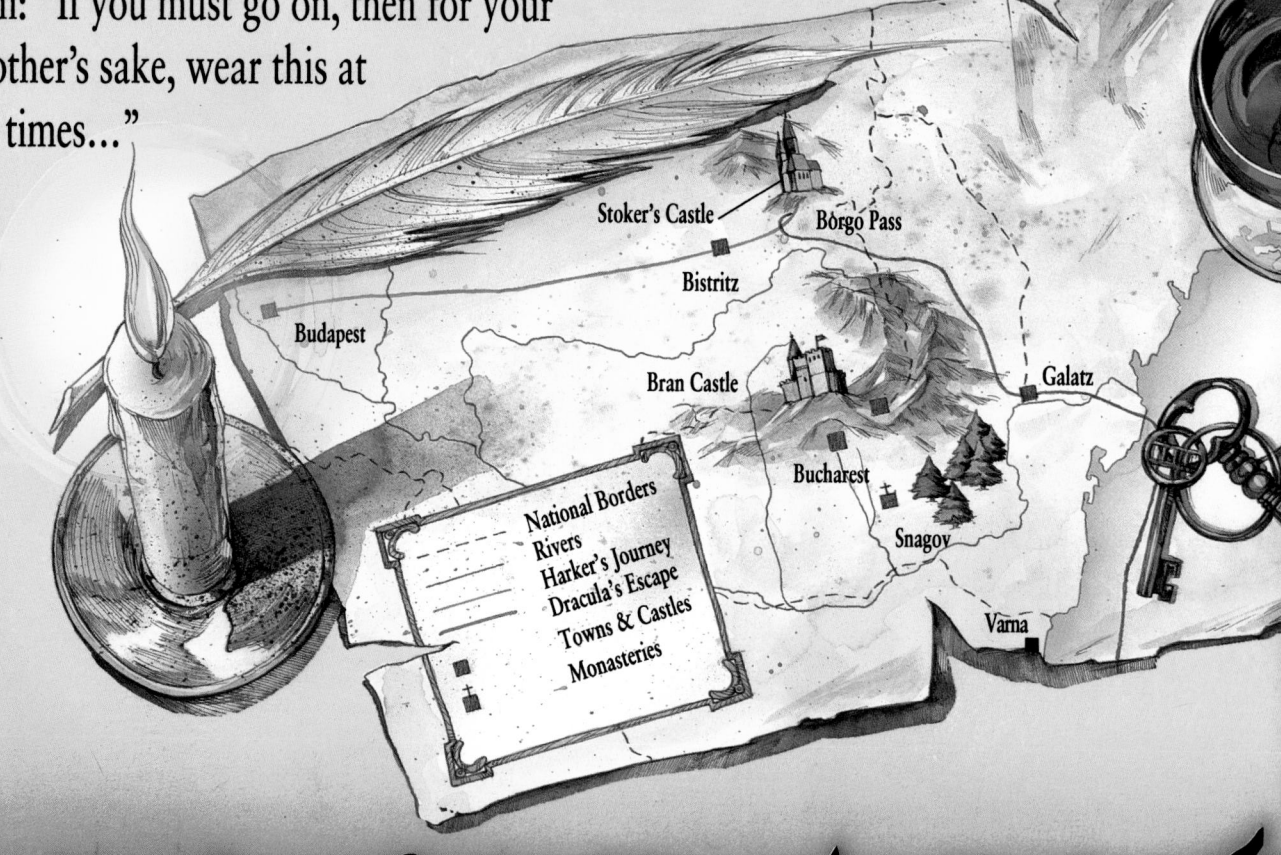

Stoker's Castle
Borgo Pass
Bistritz
Budapest
Bran Castle
Galatz
Bucharest
Snagov
Vama

National Borders
Rivers
Harker's Journey
Dracula's Escape
Towns & Castles
Monasteries

HOME TO VAMPIRES

Transylvania, the home of Dracula, is a land of great beauty. It is also a place of mystery, with dark forests and the lofty Carpathian Mountains to the east.

Dracula's Castle

The spooky Bran Castle (*right*) is perched high above the Transylvanian countryside. Built in 1377, it was one of Prince Vlad's (see page 11) many homes. When Stoker saw a painting of Bran Castle, he decided to base Dracula's

castle on it. However, Stoker placed his fictional castle far from the real castles (see story map, *left*).

To the south, the mysterious island of Snagov sits on a lake hidden by dense forests. According to legend, Vlad was buried here, but his remains have never been found!

The Land Over the Forest

In the late 1890s, the time of the story, Transylvania (*above left*) was part of Austria-Hungary, a huge empire stretching from Switzerland to Russia (*see map below*). Today, it is in northwestern Romania. In the past, dense forests dominated the countryside so much that medieval writers gave the region its name, "trans-silva," which in Latin means "over the forest."

These forests created a perfect haven for superstitious beliefs. Even today, local villagers believe that the forces of good and evil are constantly in battle, and place crosses by the roadside to protect the fields and passing travelers.

As the coach reached the Borgo Pass, the horses began to rear and snort wildly. Another coach, as black as the night, screeched into view. It was driven by a tall ma with a great black hat and eyes that gleamed red in the light of the lamps. The other passengers made the sign of the cross as Harker climbed in. The driver took his bags, and with a show of incredible strength, tossed them onto the coach. Then, with a crack of his whip, they plunged into the night.

The coach rattled along the narrow track, bordered by trees on one side and a rocky cliff on the other. The baying of wolves, once distant, sounded closer and closer. There, to the left, was a flickering blue flame. The driver noticed, but seemed to ignore it.

A few minutes later, the coach came to a sudden halt. Looking out, Harker froze in terror. They had been surrounded by a pack of hungry wolves. The driver leapt to the ground and, with a sweep of his arm, commanded them to go. All at once, they vanished into the night. Overcome by fear, Harker was unable to speak or move...

PEASANT OR COUNT?

Bram Stoker's *Dracula* is full of Transylvanian folklore. One example is the legend of St. George's Eve (April 22). On this night, evil was said to be at its most powerful, as the woman warns Harker in the story. It was also said to be the best time for finding buried treasures, because on that night they burn with an eerie blue flame.

Stoker's Count (*below, right*), however, is very different from traditional vampires. He is an elegant nobleman, with a pale, handsome face. He is also clean-shaven – apart from his mustache. In contrast, Transylvanian vampires (*below, left*) were rough creatures with bellowing voices and bright red faces covered in stubble!

In the book, Dracula enjoys sinking his teeth into ladies' necks. In folklore, vampires hurled themselves at their victims' chests, smothering them to death. Folklore vampires were also less fussy about their victims – they were known to feast on cows' and pigs' blood!

When he awoke, Harker found himself in the courtyard of an ancient castle. As soon as he stepped out of the carriage it vanished down a dark alley. Turning, Harker faced a huge wooden door studded with iron nails. He patiently waited. And waited. But nobody came as he shivered in the icy Carpathian air. Then, just as he had given up hope, came the sound of approaching footsteps and the clanking of massive bolts being drawn back. The door creaked slowly open. There stood a tall, handsome man, clad in black from head to foot. In fact, he looked suspiciously like the mystery coachman. "Count Dracula...?" asked Harker nervously.

"Yes, I am Dracula. Welcome to my house. Enter freely and of your own will." Puzzled by this strange welcome, Harker stepped across the threshold. The Count led his hungry guest into a large dining room. In the corner, a mighty fire roared up the chimney. Harker's eye was drawn to a painting above the fireplace. "Ah, I see you have noticed my great ancestor Vlad V, defender of his people."

VLAD THE IMPALER

The man in the painting is actually Dracula himself! The Count that Harker meets is four hundred years old. Stoker borrowed from legends about Prince Vlad (*left*), a Romanian hero who defended his country against Turkish invaders. This prince's father had been a knight of the Order of the Dragon, so local people called him "Dracul," which means "dragon," and his son "Dracul-a" ("a" means "son of" in Romanian). Knights of the Dragon wore black cloaks, which Stoker used in his story.

A Real Terror!

The real Dracula, Vlad V of Wallachia (1431-1476), was famed for his cruelty. Once, visiting ambassadors forgot to take their turbans off to him – so Vlad nailed them to their heads!

Stake Out

Vlad is most famous for building a "forest of the impaled" at the border of his kingdom. Sharp stakes were speared through the bodies of countless enemies as a warning to those who dared to attack him (*left*). This earned him the nickname "Tepes," meaning "impaler."

To be fair, many stories were made up by enemies like the Turkish Sultan Mehmet II (*above*). But Vlad was never called a vampire – it was Stoker who made him into one.

For some reason, the Count wasn't hungry, but Harker plunged into the delicious food before him while they looked at the papers for Carfax House.

After dinner, Dracula led his guest to his room. "You may go anywhere in my castle," said the Count, "except where the doors are locked, where of course you will not wish to go." With a wicked smile, he swept into the night.

The next day, Harker found breakfast waiting for him, but no Dracula. Evening came, and still he had not appeared. Harker went to his window to see if anyone was in the Count's rooms below. What he saw made his blood run cold.

The Count's body slowly emerged from the window. As he began to crawl down the castle walls, his cloak spread out like the wings of a giant bat...

BAT IN A FLAP!

Count Dracula climbing down the castle walls must have been a terrible sight, but as late as the 18th century, similar sights were not uncommon!

The Early Flappers

In 1742, the Marquis of Bacqueville attached wings to his arms and legs, and leapt from a tall building in an attempt to cross the Seine River. He crashed into a barge, breaking both legs! He didn't realize that human muscles are too weak to carry the human body. In fact, we would need shoulders 7 feet wide to house muscles powerful enough to fly!

Incredible Contraptions

In the 15th century, Leonardo da Vinci took a serious look at the problem of flight. His sketches (*right*) show that he was thinking of a machine called an ornithopter, which copied the flapping action of bats and birds.

Later inventors followed him with some amazing devices (*left*). All were doomed to failure, as they didn't realize that the shape of an animal's wing helps to keep it in the air.

The following night, Harker again saw the Count creeping down the castle walls. This time he seemed to disappear into thin air, and moments later a bat fluttered where the Count had been.

Certain that Dracula had left the castle, Harker explored it more thoroughly than the day before. He entered even those parts forbidden to him by the Count, trying every room, every window, every door. But there was no way out.

In the candlelight, Harker could see his own footsteps in the dust, and realized he had been walking in circles. Exhausted, he collapsed into a deep sleep. The sound of gentle laughter broke the silence of his dream. In the moonlight stood three young women. All three had the brilliant white teeth and dark, piercing eyes of the Count.

They moved toward him, whispering to each other. Harker could feel his spine tingle, but his feet were fixed as if by a spell. One of the three held Harker in a grip of iron and, arching her neck backwards, brought her gaping mouth down upon him...

THE KISS OF DEATH

Many legendary demons were female spirits that attacked in the night. Several were vampires like the women in Dracula's castle. The word nightmare itself comes from an Anglo-Saxon demon called *mara*, who smothered her victims to death.

Bloody Bathtime

The most famous real-life female vampire was Elizabeth Bathory (1560-1614, *top*), a Hungarian noblewoman who became known as the "Bloody Countess." She was convinced that blood made her younger and healthier, and some accounts say as many as 650 people were killed to allow her to drink and bathe (*above*) in the blood of her victims.

Love at First Bite

One of the earliest female vampires in folklore was the Lamia (*left*). According to legend, she was a North African princess whose children were killed by the goddess Hera. In revenge, she roamed the world, sucking the blood of badly behaved children. Other stories tell how she used her beauty to lure men and then devour them.

Further east, the Indian goddess Kali (*right*) is linked to death, plagues, and blood. She is said to have drunk the blood of a rival god, Raktavija, after defeating him. She is also famous for her four arms!

Dracula appeared from nowhere, his eyes blazing. With a giant's strength, he flung Harker's attacker to one side, crying, "How dare you touch him, he is mine!" At these words, Harker fell senseless to the floor.

He recovered to find himself back in his own room. Had all this been a dream? But there was no time to think. Climbing out of the window, he inched his way down the wall and swung into the room below. The Count was nowhere to be seen.

Harker rampaged through the room, desperate for a way out of this cursed prison. Finally, as all hope had left him, he felt a gentle breeze. A secret door! Terrified but determined, he tiptoed along a dark, damp passage to a crypt. The smell of death was everywhere.

At the center of the crypt lay a great coffin. Harker had to look. With a terrible creak, he pulled open the lid...Dracula! There the hideous creature lay, smiling in satisfaction. From a corner of his mouth ran a scarlet trickle of fresh blood. Screaming, Harker ran as fast as his strength would allow.

BLOODSUCKERS

Bloodsuckers aren't always as terrifying as the Prince of Darkness – and many of them, like the fleas on your dog, share a house with you. Here are two notorious animal bloodsuckers:

Little Suckers

The mosquito (*below*) is perhaps the best known of the

insect bloodsuckers. It feels for a suitable place to pierce the skin with the soft labium that surrounds its "needle." Then it stabs its prey and pumps in digestive fluids before sipping blood out.

eye

needle

antennae

labium

Vampire Worms

Next time you wade up an innocent-looking stream, watch out for another tiny vampire – the leech. This shiny worm (*left*) clings to its prey using a sucker, makes a wound, and then sucks out the blood.

Leeches were once believed to cure everything from headaches to being overweight. They were attached all over the patient's body (*right*). The leeches were harvested by people who waded into ponds and used their legs as bait! Today, doctors are again using this remarkable creature. Leeches help to heal reattached limbs because a chemical in their saliva stops blood from clotting.

Jonathan Harker's wife Mina stood on the cliffs, high above the fishing town of Whitby. Why hadn't Jonathan written to her from Castle Dracula? As she gazed hopefully out to sea, she felt a storm brewing in the air. All the boats in the bay headed quickly for the safety of the port – except one, a mysterious schooner. If Mina had only known what was on board that ghostly ship.

Three weeks earlier, Dracula had left Jonathan among the castle's hidden secrets and had set off for London, seeking fresh victims. He had arranged for fifty boxes filled with Transylvanian soil to be loaded onto a ship. As it sailed to England, he crept from his hidden coffin and feasted upon the crew.

Nearing the coast, Dracula cried out to the powerful forces of darkness. This was the storm that Mina felt. It hurled the ship against the rocks with a great crash. As it sank, a huge white wolf leapt ashore. The next day, a coast guard found the ship's captain still tied to the wheel, his throat ripped out...

VAMPIRE ANIMALS

Most people associate bats with vampires, but according to European folklore, almost any creature could become a vampire, including wolves (such as that in Stoker's story), sheep, chickens, and even butterflies! During the Middle Ages, cats were thought to have direct links with the devil. So when the vampire plagues of the 17th and 18th centuries swept across Europe (see page 33), cats were again linked with the forces of evil.

Beware the Bajang

Vampire cats were also common in the Far East. The Malaysian Bajang appeared as a polecat, and normally chased after children. However, it could be imprisoned and kept in a tabong, a vessel made of bamboo closed by a stopper made from special leaves. Children were protected from the mischievous Bajang by amulets (magic charms, *top*) hung around their necks.

Real polecats are actually relatives of the weasel. About 30 inches long, they live in the woods and forests of Asia, Europe, and North Africa. Like bats, they are creatures of the night – perhaps this is why they were also thought to be demons.

Nabeshima, the Vampire Cat

Legend has it that this Japanese demon (*right*) strangled a woman named O Toyo, then took on her shape. The catwoman fed on a local prince during the night, who became weaker and weaker. Eventually, the demon cat was discovered and slain in a great hunt through the mountains. The cat was seen again in 1929, so who knows...

The great white wolf pressed its face against the window. Inside, no one saw. Lucy Westenra was far too busy enjoying the company – three handsome men sat opposite – competing for her attention. On the left sat the tall American, Quincey Morris. Next to him sat Lucy's future husband, Lord Arthur Holmwood and finally, Jack Seward, the family doctor. This was Lucy's engagement party, and she and her dear friend Mina were going to enjoy it! Unfortunately, the wolf had other plans for Lucy.

That night, the sleeping Lucy was drawn onto the clifftops in a trance. The sound of a banging door woke Mina and Dr. Seward, who desperately searched for their friend in the heavy sea fog. A huge bat fluttered out of the mist, and frightened them. Then they saw Lucy's body, collapsed in a heap on the ground.

Dr. Seward carried her inside. Examining Lucy, he looked confused: "I just can't understand what's happened to her. There's only one person who might be able to help us – Professor Abraham Van Helsing."

COMPLETELY BATS

Long before Dracula was written, bats had a reputation for evil. Perhaps this was because they emerge at night, when the devil was thought to be at work. But this belief is very European – in China and the Middle East, bats are lucky animals. Anyway, even vampire bats pose little threat to humans. Yet, due to ignorance and stories like Dracula, they are still hunted ruthlessly around the world.

Weird & Wonderful

There are an amazing 950 species of bat, living in every environment from the islands of the Pacific to the forests of Northern Europe. They range in size from the 6 inch (16 cm) Kitti's hog-nosed bat to the giant Samoan Flying Fox, with its wing span of 7 feet (2 m). Most bats eat fruit (*top*) and insects, though some specialize in catching small rodents or fish. They all have hooklike feet that allow them to hang upside down. Many species live in colonies, some of up to 50 million bats. Together they eat about 250 tons of insects each night!

Night Hunters

Bats have a remarkable ability to fly and catch insects in the dark. They do this by squeaking at a very high pitch. The sound waves sent out reflect off the prey and return to the bat (*right*). Many bats have developed enlarged, folded ears to pick up the sounds clearly.

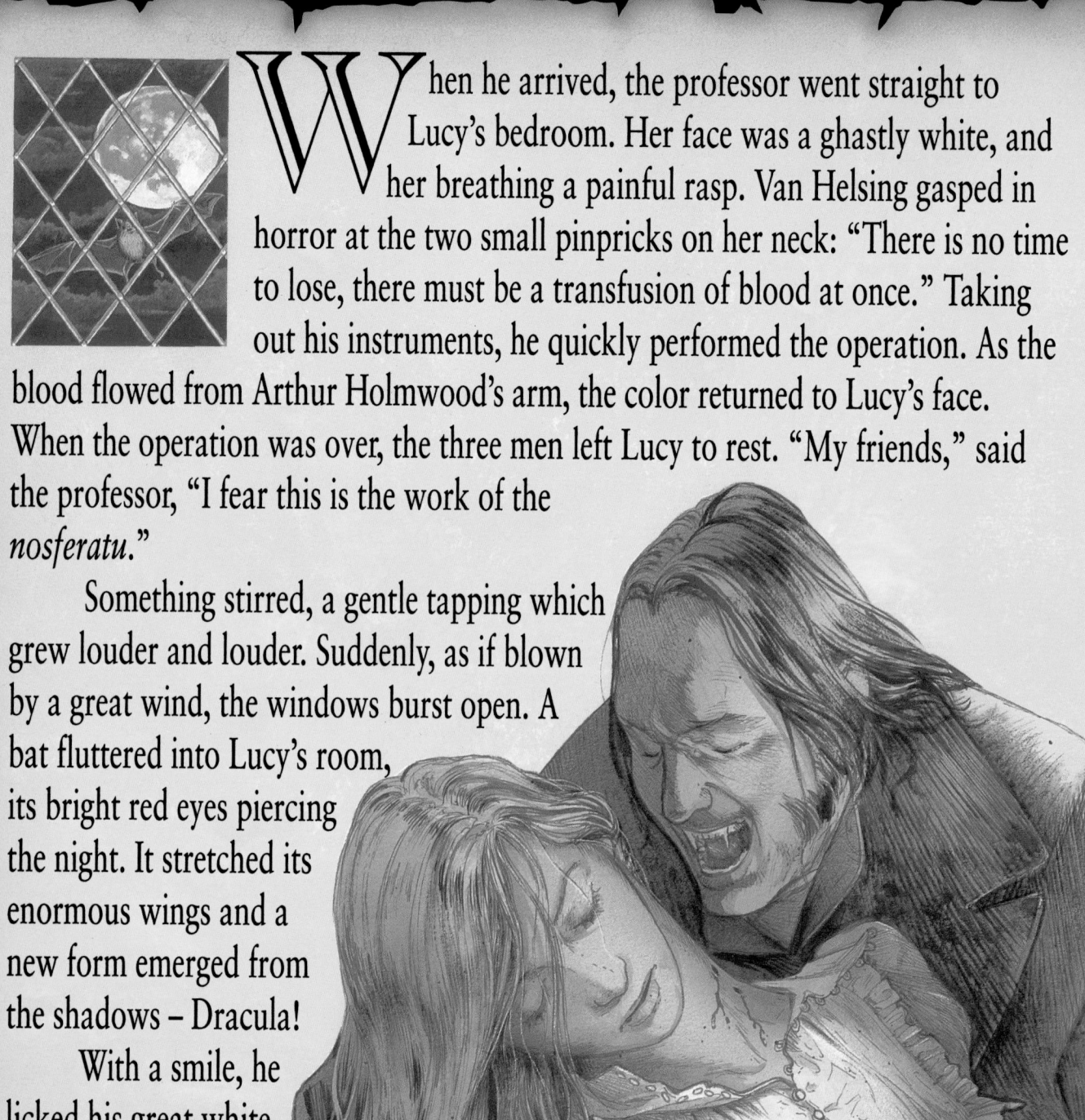

When he arrived, the professor went straight to Lucy's bedroom. Her face was a ghastly white, and her breathing a painful rasp. Van Helsing gasped in horror at the two small pinpricks on her neck: "There is no time to lose, there must be a transfusion of blood at once." Taking out his instruments, he quickly performed the operation. As the blood flowed from Arthur Holmwood's arm, the color returned to Lucy's face. When the operation was over, the three men left Lucy to rest. "My friends," said the professor, "I fear this is the work of the *nosferatu.*"

Something stirred, a gentle tapping which grew louder and louder. Suddenly, as if blown by a great wind, the windows burst open. A bat fluttered into Lucy's room, its bright red eyes piercing the night. It stretched its enormous wings and a new form emerged from the shadows – Dracula!

With a smile, he licked his great white fangs, then sank them deep into Lucy's throat.

FANTASTIC FANGS!

When you think of Dracula you think of bats, but the folklore vampires of Eastern Europe were never linked to these flying mammals. However, when Bram Stoker heard about the bloodsucking bats from South America, it's easy to see why he wanted to include them in his story.

Midnight Snacks

Vampire bats are shy, nervous animals – not at all like the Prince of Darkness! They usually land near their prey, then crawl or hop up to it (*above*). Using their sharp, pointed teeth, the bats bite any part of the victim that is soft and fleshy (such as the neck of a horse, *right*). These teeth are huge compared to the size of the skull (*left*). Instead of sucking out the blood (like Dracula), the bats lap it up with their tongues as a cat would with milk. Special chemicals in their saliva help to keep the blood flowing. They also flap their wings rapidly to keep their victim cool (and asleep!) as they drink.

Have a Drink on Me

While Dracula enjoys a long drink from his victims, vampire bats drink hardly any blood at all. They weigh only about 1 ounce, and half a quart of blood would be enough to keep a bat going for over a month. Sometimes, if they drink too much blood they get too heavy to take off again! They mostly feed from animals such as pigs – only rarely do they attack humans.

Lucy became weaker and weaker as Dracula continued his nightly visits. Meanwhile, Mina received news of her beloved husband. A letter had come from the Sister Superior of a remote Transylvanian convent, where Jonathan lay sick with a violent fever.

The day Harker discovered Dracula's gruesome resting place, some men had come to remove the boxes of soil from the castle. Harker hid, watching as they nailed down the lid of Dracula's coffin and placed it among the boxes.

He knew he would not survive the night if the women who attacked him were as terrifyingly real as the Count. He saw his opportunity and raced through the open door.

Driven by fear, Harker ran until he thought his lungs would burst. All around, hungry eyes watched him from the trees. Then, as night fell, he saw a light in the distance – safety at last! Reaching the convent door, he collapsed into an exhausted sleep.

KNOW ANY VAMPIRES?

How can you tell if someone is a vampire? Look around you – do any of your friends have red eyes, long nails, hairy palms, and a hatred of bright lights? To double-check, hold up a mirror. If the person has no reflection, then run for it!

Five Ways To Protect Yourself Against Vampires

If you think you've detected a vampire, here are some good ways to protect yourself:

Garlic ✚ Used on all windows and doors, around the neck, and even under the arms!

Crucifixes or crosses ✚ Traditional favorites for keeping vampires away.

Holy water or wafers ✚ These burn vampire skin.

Seeds ✚ Mustard and poppy seeds should be sprinkled along corridors.

Tar ✚ Paint crosses on all doors with tar.

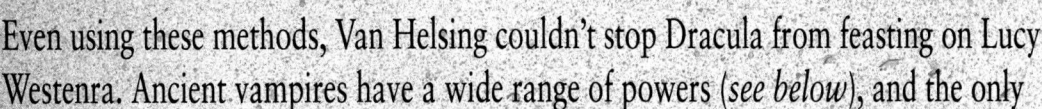

Even using these methods, Van Helsing couldn't stop Dracula from feasting on Lucy Westenra. Ancient vampires have a wide range of powers (*see below*), and the only sure way to stop them from pestering you is to dig them up and kill them (*above*).

The Powers of Darkness

Strength ✚ Equal to many men. Increases with age.
Power over nature ✚ Vampires control wind and rain. *Turning to mist* ✚ To get through tiny cracks.
Creating other vampires ✚ It only takes three bites!

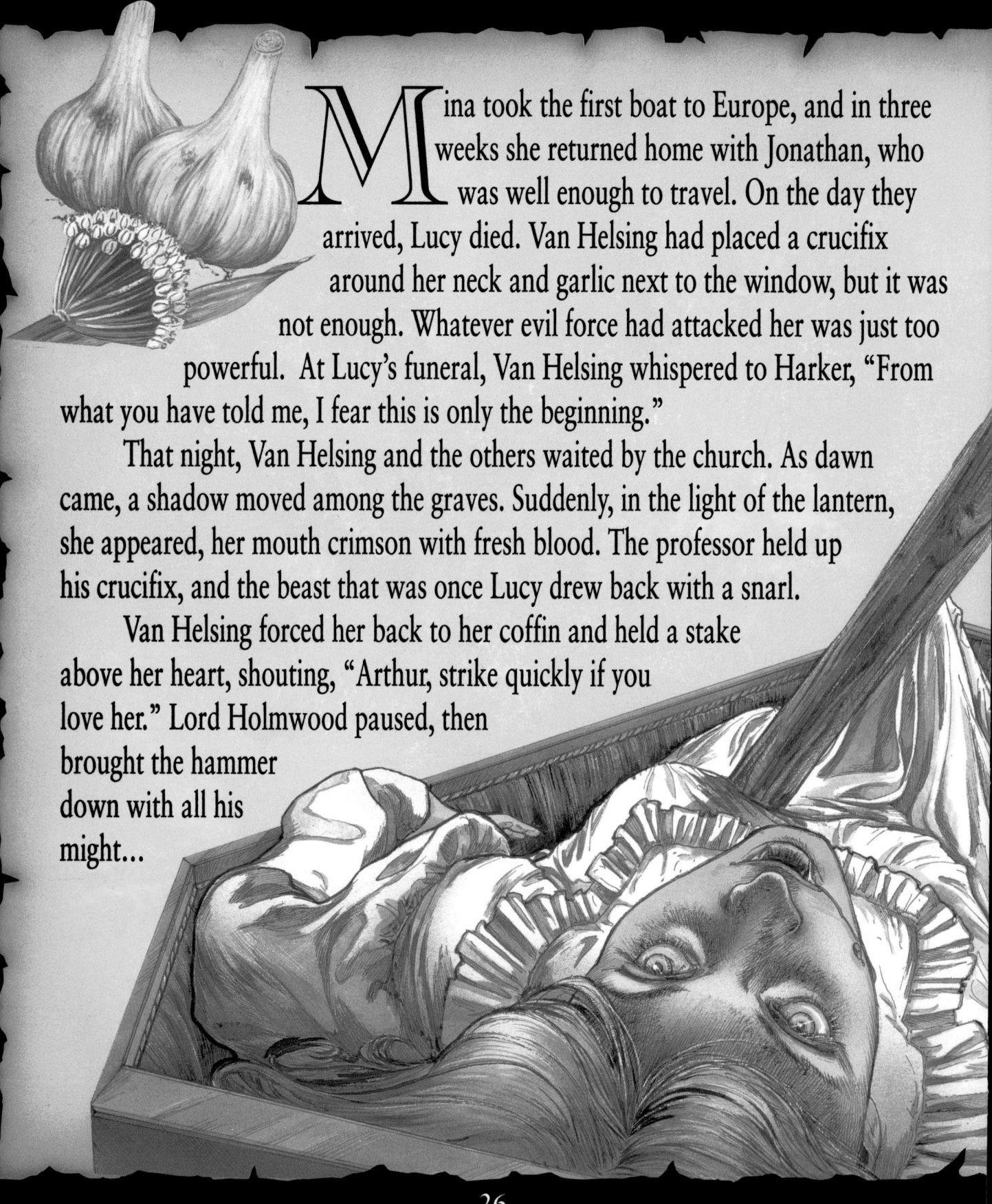

Mina took the first boat to Europe, and in three weeks she returned home with Jonathan, who was well enough to travel. On the day they arrived, Lucy died. Van Helsing had placed a crucifix around her neck and garlic next to the window, but it was not enough. Whatever evil force had attacked her was just too powerful. At Lucy's funeral, Van Helsing whispered to Harker, "From what you have told me, I fear this is only the beginning."

That night, Van Helsing and the others waited by the church. As dawn came, a shadow moved among the graves. Suddenly, in the light of the lantern, she appeared, her mouth crimson with fresh blood. The professor held up his crucifix, and the beast that was once Lucy drew back with a snarl.

Van Helsing forced her back to her coffin and held a stake above her heart, shouting, "Arthur, strike quickly if you love her." Lord Holmwood paused, then brought the hammer down with all his might...

FIGHTING DRACULA

Professor Van Helsing uses a stake to finish off Lucy
Westenra, but this is just one of many ways of destroying an unwelcome *nosferatu*.
Different methods are used for vampires in different parts of the world, and
care must be taken not to get them mixed up! Here are a few, some
common, some not so common:

Touching with a crucifix – Only works on young vampires.
Stealing the left sock (left) – Useful for some species only. Fill
with soil and throw it in a river.

Sunlight – Be careful, as this doesn't always work with old vampires like Dracula.
Cremation – An old favorite that works equally well anywhere in the world.
Bottling – Works for Malaysian vampires, but it's best to hire a sorcerer for this one.
Extracting and boiling the heart – Not recommended, as it can be very messy!
Piercing with a sword (top of page) – Remember to get your sword blessed first.

Trapping in the grave – For the best-smelling results,
use dog roses (*left*) to trap your
vampire. However, sticky rice is
a must for all Chinese vampires.

The Vampire Hunter's Kit

No vampire hunter should leave home without the
following tools of the trade:
stakes ⚬⚬ mallet ⚬⚬ pistol ⚬⚬ rope ⚬⚬ crowbar
flashlight ⚬⚬ mirror ⚬⚬ knives ⚬⚬ garlic
saw ⚬⚬ holy wafer ⚬⚬ crucifix ⚬⚬ holy water

Returning from the graveyard, the friends gathered in the study. Van Helsing spoke: "Dracula is *nosferatu*, one of the undead, a vampire. Vampires have lived across the world since the beginning of time, and their powers are strong. We cannot rest until Dracula has been destroyed. First, we must find the fifty boxes in which he sleeps. We should start with Carfax House, the Count's new London home. Can you take us there, Jonathan?"

Just then, a shot rang out and the window shattered. A few seconds later, a breathless Quincey Morris ran into the room. "Sorry to scare you, but I saw a huge bat sitting outside and took a shot at it, without any luck." Van Helsing knew then that there was no time to lose. The following day, the group took the first train to London, staying at Dr. Seward's house.

As evening came, Jonathan stood guard outside. But he never noticed the thick green mist drifting toward the house. The evil fog crept up the walls and slipped through the crack under Mina's window. The next morning, Mina Harker found two small marks on her neck...

THE WORLD OF THE UNDEAD

The vampire that Van Helsing describes to the others is based on Transylvanian folktales. However, very different vampire stories have existed in other parts of the world for centuries. Here are some of the more unusual ones:

All Shapes and Sizes!

The Malaysian langsuir flies at night in the form of an owl (*left*). By day, it appears as a woman with incredibly long nails and bright green robes. To stop it, you must cut its nails, then force its hair into a hole in its neck, which it normally uses to drink the blood of children! Another Malaysian vampire, the polong, looks like a tiny female no bigger than the top joint of the little finger. This bottled imp (*above*) attacks at its owner's command, afflicting the victim with a strange disease.

Vampire Monsters

In 1784, a huge vampire terrorized cattle farmers in Chile. However, this vampire was rather different from Dracula – it was a cross between a giant bat, a lion, and a human being (right)!

In China, the most feared vampire was known as the Kwang-shi. These large demons had glaring red eyes, sharp fangs and talons, and were covered in a thich coat of green hair (left).

Arriving at Carfax House, the group spread out in search of Dracula's boxes. The vast house was thick with dust, the air stagnant and foul. When they reached the chapel, Quincey Morris jumped back in horror. The whole place was alive with rats. But with several sharp blows on Arthur Holmwood's whistle, his three terriers bounded into the house. The dogs sent swarms of rats scurrying left and right, and in minutes the chapel was clear. Twenty-nine boxes were found, and Van Helsing destroyed each one with a few drops of holy water.

That night, while Van Helsing plotted with Quincey and Arthur, they heard a sudden noise. They raced upstairs to Mina's room and found the Count towering over Mina, his lips dripping with blood, his eyes red and ablaze with hate. On the other side of the room, Jonathan sat helplessly in a chair, hypnotized by Dracula.

Van Helsing took out his cross, making the Count step back in fear. A great cloud passed in front of the moon, and when Quincey struck a match, Dracula was gone.

LOOK INTO MY EYES

In Bram Stoker's story, Dracula puts women (and Jonathan Harker) under his spell with a glance. But how does hypnosis really work?

The Mystery of Hypnosis

Named after *Hypnos*, the Greek god of sleep (*right*), *hypnosis* is when someone's commands and actions make you fall asleep. No one is quite sure how it works, but some scientists think that under hypnosis the left side of the brain (involved in logic) is turned off. This is achieved by fixing the mind of the subject on something like a swinging watch (*above*) or a soothing voice.

This leaves the right side of the brain, the creative side, free to do what it likes! Though hypnosis is best known for the amusing things it can make people do, it is also used to perform operations without the need for painkilling drugs.

The First Hypnotist

Dr. Franz Mesmer (*left*) first introduced hypnosis as a revolutionary new healing method in 1774. He put his patients in tubs of water while he walked around the room in a purple suit, touching them with an iron wand! He believed a magnetic current, or "animal magnetism," ran through the body, so he attached magnets to various parts of the patient. Though Mesmer's theories were later proved wrong, the word "mesmerized" is still used to mean hypnotized.

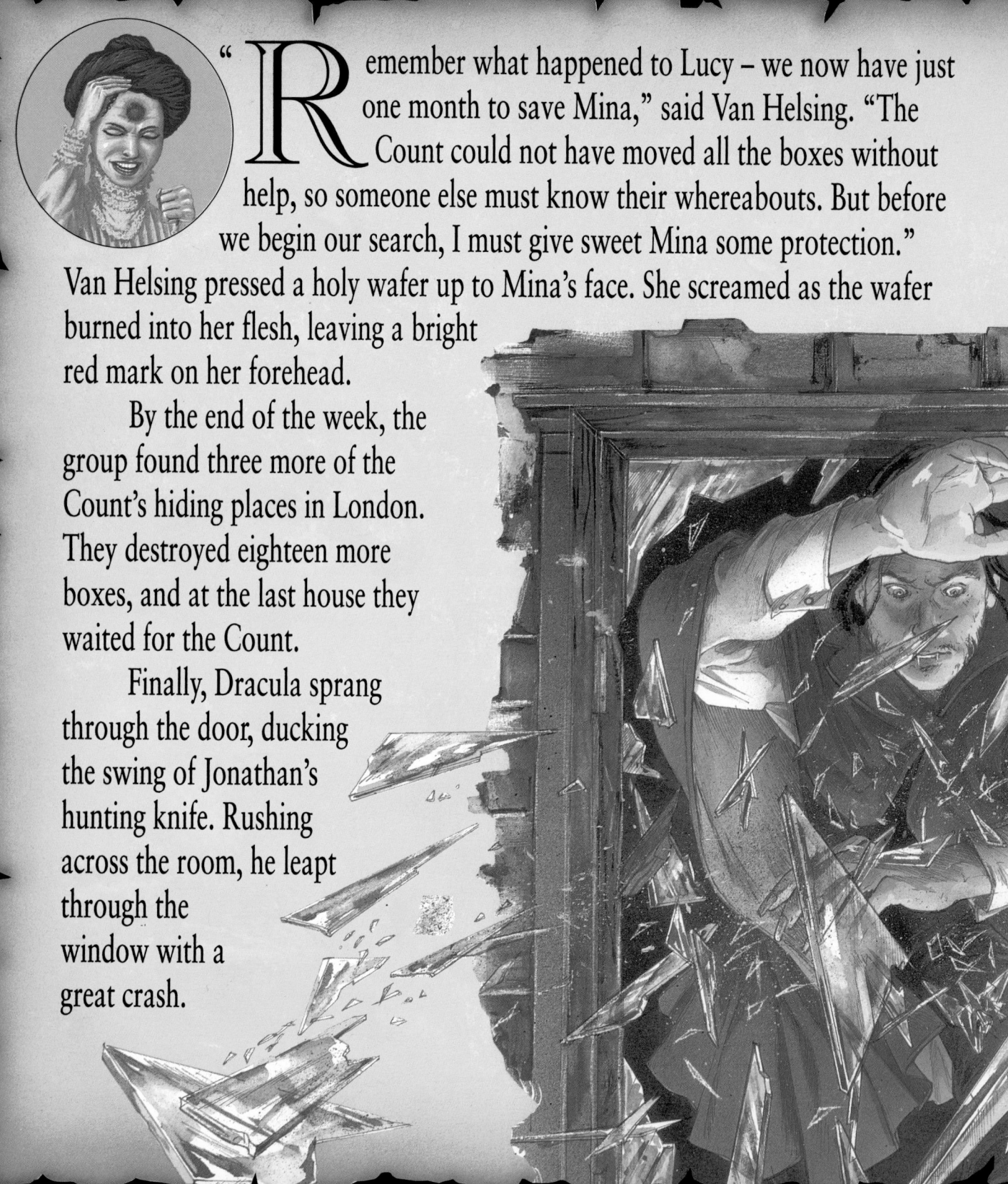

"Remember what happened to Lucy – we now have just one month to save Mina," said Van Helsing. "The Count could not have moved all the boxes without help, so someone else must know their whereabouts. But before we begin our search, I must give sweet Mina some protection."

Van Helsing pressed a holy wafer up to Mina's face. She screamed as the wafer burned into her flesh, leaving a bright red mark on her forehead.

By the end of the week, the group found three more of the Count's hiding places in London. They destroyed eighteen more boxes, and at the last house they waited for the Count.

Finally, Dracula sprang through the door, ducking the swing of Jonathan's hunting knife. Rushing across the room, he leapt through the window with a great crash.

DO VAMPIRES EXIST?

In the 17th and 18th centuries, a series of vampire plagues swept through Europe. Entire regions lived in terror of vampires like Arnold Paole (*right*). Paole's corpse was dug up intact in 1732, four years after his death. His jaw was open and his body was swollen with fresh blood.

Premature Burial

Before doctors understood how plagues occur, they were seen as a magical curse. During the Black Death in the 14th century, special witch doctors tried to cure people using magical potions and strange ceremonies (*left*).

By the 17th century, plagues were being linked to vampires. With so many people dying, some were accidentally buried while still alive! So when their coffins were dug up, their bodies would seem much fresher than they should be, and they might be bloody from trying to escape. Also, due to the effects of the plague, they would have white skin and bright red gums – just like vampires were supposed to.

Mad Dog's Disease?

One theory is that vampires were people infected by rabid dogs (right), because victims of rabies start to act like animals, even biting other people! In the end, however, most vampire myths are probably due to superstition. But if you met a tall man with sharp, pointed teeth on a dark night, would you stop to find out?

With only three coffins left, Van Helsing knew that Dracula could not risk staying in London. "He will return to Transylvania to recover his strength, and we must follow him." At the docks, Arthur found out that only one ship set sail for the Black Sea, the *Czarina Catherine*, bound for the port of Varna. Dracula had to be on it.

After sailing across the English Channel, the friends caught the Orient Express to Varna. They would arrive one week ahead of Dracula. But the *Czarina Catherine* never arrived in Varna. It had been swept by powerful winds to Galatz, further up the coast. "We must split into groups," said Mina. "Quincey and Dr. Seward, you follow him on horseback. Arthur and Jonathan, use a fast boat along the canals. Dr. Van Helsing and I will travel by train and coach to the Borgo Pass."

MOVIE DRACULAS

Dracula and his vampire friends have been baring their fangs on screen for over 70 years. To date, over 300 vampire films have been made worldwide!

Classic Silver Screen Draculas

The makers of the first major Dracula film were forced to call the film *Nosferatu* (1922, *top*) because Bram Stoker's wife, Florence, didn't want the film made. Though it was made in the era of silent movies, it influenced many later films.

The classic *Dracula* of 1931 starred Bela Lugosi, a Hungarian actor whose haunting voice brought the role of Dracula to life. Christopher Lee (*second from top*) showed a new level of gore in the 1950s.

Modern Draculas

Recent films like *The Hunger* (1983, *third down*) have featured many new vampires, but Stoker's story was popular enough to be remade in 1992 (*left*).

After a week of hot pursuit across Romania, none of the groups had caught up with the Count. Van Helsing and Mina were the first to reach the Borgo Pass. That night, as they sat by the campfire, Mina laughed wickedly. Van Helsing turned to see the three women from Jonathan's dream. They called to Mina: "Come, sister, you are one of us." But the professor had placed holy wafers in a circle around the camp, and Mina could no more join them than they could approach. Howling with anger, they melted into the night.

At dawn, Van Helsing climbed up to the castle. Remembering Jonathan's description, he made his way down to the crypt. Where Dracula's coffin had once been, there lay the three vampires. This was no time for mercy. The professor cut off each head with a single mighty blow, and waited for the Count.

As the sun began to set, a coach carrying Dracula's coffin appeared on the horizon. Driving the carriage was a terrifying team of heavily-armed bandits. How was Van Helsing to stop them alone?

CRAZY VAMPIRES

The story of Dracula helped to create a whole world of amazing vampire creatures, from the cartoon character Count Duckula (*left*) to vampire cars and motorcycles. Among the most peculiar variations on the vampire theme are bloodthirsty killer plants.

Wild Watermelons!

According to the Muslim gypsies of Bosnia, both watermelons (*right*) and pumpkins can become vampires if they are kept for more than ten days after Christmas. Stained with blood, they are said to growl and roll around pestering the living.

Many films have starred cannibal plants. In the 1986 musical comedy *Little Shop of Horrors*, a florist's assistant creates a carnivorous talking plant (*below*) and must murder people in order to feed it.

Green and Deadly

Luckily for us, the real-life carnivorous plant Venus's-flytrap only grows to about 1 foot high! This remarkable plant (*below*) found in North America grows in nitrogen-starved soil, so it eats insects to make up the extra minerals. On each leaf is a set of sensitive hairs. When an insect touches these hairs, it triggers the two leaves, which immediately close like a trap and hold the insect inside.

The soft parts of the insect are digested by a fluid made by special glands in the leaf. After the plant has taken in the food, the trap opens and the leaf is ready to capture another victim. When a leaf has caught several insects, it withers and dies.

"Look! Look!," shouted Mina. About a mile behind the carriage were Quincey and Dr. Seward, riding at breakneck speed. Suddenly, Jonathan and Arthur dashed out from the forest crying, "Halt!"

The bandit leader saw them and urged the carriage onward, as his gang blocked their way. Quincey and Jonathan forced a route through them, leapt onto the carriage, and pushed the huge coffin to the ground. Quincey bravely held the bandits off with his great bowie knife, but in the dying sunlight Mina could see that their flashing blades had wounded him badly.

Arthur and Dr. Seward pulled out their rifles and the bandits knew they were beaten. Jonathan pried open the coffin lid with his knife, and there lay Dracula. He saw the sinking sun, and his red eyes gleamed with triumph. But one sweep of Jonathan's knife ripped his throat in two, and Quincey plunged the bowie into his heart. Before their eyes, the evil body crumbled into dust.

With this final effort, Quincey collapsed. He died pointing at Mina, gasping, "See, the mark of Dracula has gone. I have not died in vain."

VAMPIRE LANGUAGE

Amulets – Anything worn as a charm against evil (like a rabbit's foot).

Animal Magnetism – Mesmer's theory that a magnetic current flows through the body.

Candles – *(center)* Vampires dislike all forms of light, but candles only scare off very young vampires.

Crucifix – A cross that represents the Christian image of the crucifixion.

Crypt – An underground room, sometimes used as a burial place.

Garlic – *(bottom of opposite page)* A plant used to ward off vampires.

Hypnotist – Someone who can place others into a deep sleep by his or her actions.

Nightmare – A bad dream, supposedly caused by the Anglo-Saxon demon *mara*, who sits on you as you sleep.

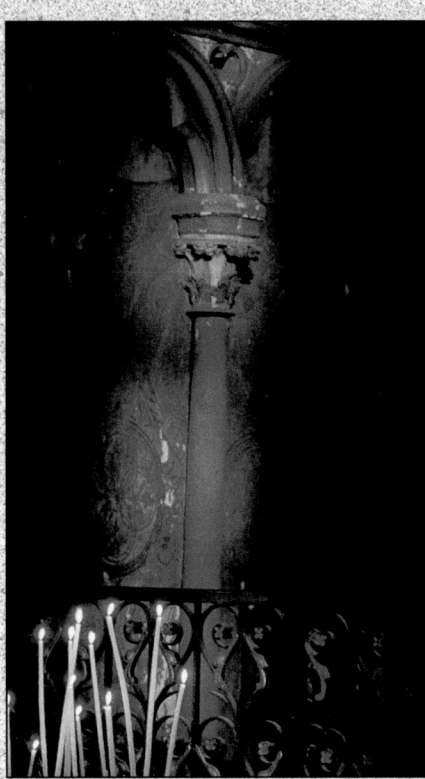

Nosferatu – A German word for the undead in general, but also a particular vampire from the Alpine mountains.

Ornithopter – A flying machine that copies the flapping motion of bats and birds to get off the ground.

Rabies – A disease common among dogs that causes madness.

Stake – A thick stick or post, usually made of wood, with a sharp point at one end for driving it into the ground (or vampires!).

Transfusion – The process of transferring the blood of one animal or human into the veins of another.

Vampire – These come in many shapes and forms, but they all live on human blood. Also known as the undead because although they are dead, they are very much alive!

INDEX

Photocredits
4, 24, 36, 37ml, 38, 39: Roger Vlitos; 5, 11t, b, 13 all, 15 both, 17bl, 25b, 31, 34: Mary Evans Picture Library; 7 both, 8, 10, 23, 25t, 35 all: Frank Spooner Pictures; 11m, 17br: Hulton Deutsch; 17t, 18, 19, 20 both, 28: Bruce Coleman Ltd; 7t: Thames TV; 37mr: Warner Bros, courtesy Kobal Collection. Key - - t=top; m=middle; b=bottom; l=left; r=right